Bible Story Hidden Pictures
Coloring & Activity Book

Written by Robin Fogle
Illustrations by Michael Denman

The purchase of this coloring book grants you the rights to photocopy the contents for classroom use.
Notice: It is unlawful to copy these pages for resale purposes. Copy permission is for private use only.

Warner
Press Kids
educate • nurture • inspire
www.warnerpress.org

Adam & Eve

(Genesis 2:4—3:24)

Adam and Eve lived in the beautiful Garden of Eden. One day the serpent tricked Eve into eating the fruit God had told her not to eat. She also gave some to Adam. Because Adam and Eve disobeyed God they had to leave the beautiful garden forever.

Find and circle 6 snakes hidden in the picture.

Noah's Ark

(Genesis 6—9:17)

God told Noah to build a huge boat called an ark. Then God told him to bring his family and two of every kind of creature into the ark. The flood came but Noah, his family and the animals were safe. When the flood was over God put a rainbow in the sky and promised never to flood the whole earth again.

Find and circle a dog bone, a leaf, a Bible and an apple hidden in the picture.

Jesus Is Baptized

(Matthew 3:13-17)

Jesus went to the Jordan River to be baptized by John. At first John didn't want to baptize Jesus because he knew Jesus was greater than he was, but Jesus said it was the right thing to do. When Jesus came out of the water, God said, "This is my Son. I am very pleased with Him."

Find and circle a duck, a fish, a fishing pole and a frog hidden in the picture.

Moses Parts the Red Sea

(Exodus 13:17—14:31)

God chose Moses to lead His people out of Egypt. They walked on and on until they came to the Red Sea. Soon the people saw the Egyptian army chasing them. They were very afraid but God told Moses to stretch his hand out over the sea. God pushed back the water until dry land appeared and the people crossed safely to the other side. The Egyptians tried to follow but God sent the water crashing back down and washed them all away.

Find and circle a brick, a dog, a Bible and a bird hidden in the picture.

Joshua & the Battle of Jericho

(Joshua 5:13—6:27)

God told Joshua it was time to capture the city of Jericho. For six days Joshua and the people marched around the city blowing trumpets. On the seventh day they marched around the city seven times. When they heard a blast from the trumpets the people gave a loud shout. The walls of Jericho collapsed to the ground, and God's people captured the city.

Find and circle a Bible, a turtle, a candle and a basket hidden in the picture.

Jesus Feeds 5,000 Men

(John 6:1-15)

Everywhere Jesus went huge crowds of people followed. One day Jesus asked Philip, "Where can we buy food for all of these people?" Philip told Jesus they didn't have enough money to buy food for everyone. Then a little boy brought Jesus his lunch of five small loaves of bread and two small fish. Jesus blessed the food and the disciples passed it out. When everyone was finished eating the disciples gathered up twelve baskets of leftovers. All the people knew they had seen a miracle.

Find and circle a lunch box, a fishing pole, a kitten and a baseball hidden in the picture.

Samson Kills a Lion

(Judges 13:1—14:6)

Samson was the strongest man in the Bible. Before he was born, God told Samson's parents he would be special. God had important work for Samson to do. One day when Samson and his parents were on their way to town a lion jumped out of the vineyards. The Spirit of the Lord gave Samson power and he killed the lion with his bare hands.

**Find and circle a pair of scissors, a sword, a loaf of bread
and a bumblebee hidden in the picture.**

God Talks to Samuel

(1 Samuel 3)

When Samuel was a little boy he lived in the temple with Eli, the priest. One night Samuel heard a voice calling him. He ran to Eli, but Eli said, "I didn't call you, Samuel. Go back to bed." This happened three times. Finally, Eli realized God was calling Samuel. He told Samuel what to say. Samuel returned to bed, and when God called again Samuel said, "Speak, Lord. Your servant is listening." God gave Samuel an important message. When Samuel grew up he did great work for God.

Find and circle a Bible, a sword, a cat and an apple hidden in the picture.

Jesus Calms the Storm

(Mark 4:35-41)

One evening Jesus and His disciples were in a boat heading towards the other side of the lake. Jesus fell asleep. Suddenly, a terrible storm came. The boat was filling with water and the disciples were afraid. They woke Jesus up and said, "Don't You care if we all drown?" Jesus got up and spoke to the wind and the waves. "Be still," He said, and the storm stopped. The disciples were amazed.

Find and circle a fish, a fishing pole, a duck and a shell hidden in the picture.

David & Goliath

(1 Samuel 17)

David was a young shepherd boy and his brothers were in the army. One day David's father sent him to check on his brothers. When David got there a giant was yelling at God's army. Everyone in the army was afraid to fight the giant. David said, "I will fight Goliath." He took his sling and gathered five smooth stones from the stream. He told the giant, "I fight you in the name of the Lord." The stone hit Goliath right between the eyes and he fell to the ground, dead.

The number 5 is hidden in six different places in the picture. Find and circle them.

The Widow's Oil

(2 Kings 4:1-7)

A wife of one of the prophets came to Elisha. "My husband is dead," she said. "Now a bill collector wants to take my two sons away to be slaves." Elisha wanted to help her. He asked what she had in her house. She said, "Nothing, except a little oil." Elisha told her to borrow as many jars as she could and to fill each one with oil. She did as he said. When all the jars were full the oil stopped flowing. She went back to Elisha who said, "Sell the oil and pay what you owe. Then you and your sons can live on the money left over."

Find and circle a dollar bill, a hat, a piggy bank and a cat hidden in the picture.

The Good Samaritan

(Luke 10:25-37)

Jesus once told the story of a man attacked and beaten by robbers who took everything he had and left him on the road. A priest and a Levite walked by but they would not help the man. Then a Samaritan came along. He saw how badly the man was hurt. The Samaritan put the man on his donkey and took him to an inn. He told the innkeeper, "Take care of him and I will pay whatever it costs when I return." Jesus used this story to help us understand how to love our neighbor.

Find and circle a mask, a hat, a money bag and a dog hidden in the picture.

Three Men in the Furnace

(Daniel 3)

The king made a huge golden statue and told all his people that they must worship it. Shadrach, Meshach and Abednego would not bow down to the statue. Evil men told the king who said to the three men, "If you don't worship my statue, you will be thrown in a fiery furnace." Shadrach, Meshach and Abednego replied, "Even if you throw us in the furnace, we will worship only God." The king had the three men thrown into the furnace. When he looked in he saw them walking around, along with a fourth man who looked like the Son of God. The king had the three men brought out of the furnace. They did not even smell like smoke. "From now on," the king said, "we will worship God."

Find and circle a Bible, a crown, a sword and a ring hidden in the picture.

Jonah & the Big Fish

(Jonah 1—4)

God told Jonah to go to Ninevah and preach but Jonah did not want to go. He got on a ship and tried to sail away from God. Soon a huge storm came. The sailors were afraid. They began asking passengers what they had done. When they came to Jonah he said, "It is my fault. I am running away from God. Throw me into the sea and the storm will stop." The sailors did as Jonah said and a big fish came and swallowed him. Immediately the storm stopped. When Jonah told God he would obey, the fish spit Jonah onto dry land.

Find and circle a flashlight, a candle, a Bible and a snorkel hidden in the picture.

The Widow's Offering

(Mark 12:41-44)

One day Jesus sat outside the temple watching people put money in the collection box. Many rich people threw in a lot of money. Then a poor widow came and put in two tiny copper coins that were worth less than a penny. Jesus told His disciples, "That poor widow has given most of all. Other people gave out of their riches but she has given all she had to live on."

Find and circle a dog, a banana, a wagon and a basketball hidden in the picture.

E4634